AF425062

dainty heart

by jason gold

dedicated to a heart

"be wistful in your knowing"

dainty heart

there are singing dashing

wonder lullaby bluffs of soft white

cloud bluffs

cloud bluffs

sky

and all the flying places

all the soaring

the birds do not look down

they look into the wind

and there are flying by moonlight

still the moonlight clouds

cloudbluffs

and this gentle feeling

of rainbow aura moon

dove soaring white wings

these tufttall billows

and these whitewave wonders

too

how they move shape

we too find our joy

in this freedom

to be our winds and to move on them

to allow movement

and to be the positive

there are singing dashing

you may read this quick

chirpsound smilebird rainbow light

mosey song innerworld genuine peace

unstill unrushed flow flow

even when a river rushes it is not even

a stressful even when boulders move

flow flow flow

rainbow lullabies

o these tufts of cloud

that show us it is

okay to become all the shapes of our heart

as we blow on the wind

to become not firm but fluidfloating

all the shapes of our heart

and a joy that soars with all the clouds

white dragon

all the beauty

all the clouds

float like

fairy grace

dainty heart

oak birds perch

pine breeze flight

magenta and it is beautiful to be fulfilled

vivid

airstreak

purple bird against blue sky

with

and all this being

all this living light

all the sunring folkarts

of any people

rooted in this earth

there are broad joys we can take

even in this era

even in this life

it is beautiful to be fulfilled

and it is beautiful to

be the sky

of all these suns

in every breath

waving water reflection of wind

waving water reflection of wind

you breeze on this clear water

an infinity to see with this mind

to perceive and such peace too

to have this mind look in the moment

all these ways

it is the wind on the surface

that presents such depth

we can allow ourselves to see

too a dancing of light

that plays this boundary

makes it real reflecting

and showing

this clear pool

forming unrigid

this moving surface

it is not unpassable

it is reflecting

but these pebbles can

splash in

or coins

likewise a fish can jump

freely

from the water

the boundary is indefinite

that is it is present but too

unforcing a separation

without keeping

should they

touch anything apart

should they touch here where the waves dance

of light too

and pass through

splashing a soundwave

into both

it is then a fountain

the spring of wonderjoy

the clear water we drink clarity

is the purity

if you can see within

if you can perceive purity within

a water or otherwise

clarity is a quality

and a revelation

we can be clear pure

perceptive of joy

pure water is more than transparent

though it is a good indication

and a flowing water is

good too

clarity and motion

transparent boundaries unhiding

not seeking to

clarity in motion

this clear ricer

and this fountain

i find such joy in

clarity in becoming

free from pollution

pure

seen and unseen

pure

this clarity

of mind and joy

flowing water

flowing pure

all this sand that runs between

all the rocks and their shining minerals

this river of purity

clarity in

mind

too

is transparent

is allowing yourself to see

is allowing your mindwater to settle

into clear see through pools

shining all this clear etheric energy of light

reflecting in your winds

but allowing you to enter

   allowing inflow

allowing a pure stream it is

unpolluted peace and pure

awareness

pollution is

sometimes clear in the water

that does not mean

there is no way to filter it

or no way to be aware of it

there is much

we can see beyond our eyes

our methods

can be personal

or collective

white rainbow cleanse white rainbow free

your words

and sight

what

would pollute

there is internal purity

and a world to celebrate

this clear water

be self determining and

happily free

crystal mind splash

in

these clear waters

we dive and swim crystal

a blowing surface of light while

a newness flows in pure

and such genuine

such willing

waving of water by the motion

as the seas rise and fall

it is a gentle boundary in that

it would not prevent your swim

among the fish

this entry into weightless

the dolphins fly from

and such a crystal water

we see in the shallows

and pure a see sea

pure a sea as the waves of this vast surface

unbroken across distances

surftiding purity and giving all this air

there is a true light

that soaks into our sea

this sun

the poetries

that spiritfall like rays

from any pen

set your language

free

there is only a freedom

formal form or style

is only a tool unlimitfree

unlimitflow and joy joy know

this anew creation freedom

is unpolluted unrestrict

is pure confident willing freelight

profident flowing with flow

a joyspring sprint

may you wash rainbow wash wave

as the wave washes over the sand

a cleansing motion

all that spiritual

floats in our sky the minds

are but expressive

there are living things

and things we bring life to poetry

both living if you open yourself

it is not production to create

in any sense

it is more intimate

more expressive and

flowing forth a energy of light

this vast

it is directed

in real time and spinning

a twirldance we live through the art

it is too an art to craft

caster and brilliant

milk and honey

purple poetries moonstone vibrations

hues and joys

shades of pink patina yellow

patina pink

all this rippling water

i find unwilling to be interfered with

myself pure unpolluted

this world is creative and

there is innate no issue

with it

collective cure

crystal waters i do swim swift

and all this kind intention of breeze

of unselfish written is pure

what i want to share

is lightknowing

this verbal art

is read to yourself word

spoken to your spirit

you imagine

receive from the word

free

all you

can

and know i do not hide things

this writing is meant to be unhidden

and accessed

and awareness i share

do not force your

reading or writing

true lights i am with you

true lights we are

and we rive

spiral

the way the energy of this planet creates spirals

all this magnetic geometry

and overarching emphasis of creation

the creationmind the spawn generation

the spawn of

a salmon river

these innate journeys

where do you feel most home

on this vast planet

is it too somewhere you've never been?

i find it is the wilderness i know is

everpresent like the stars

and i find myself watching that feeling

and find it is not being there

but knowing i am here with it

all the living expanse of living earth

how i am of its life

and undeterred

how present we will see its freedom

the people and the earth

the people of the earth

we must not be distinct or

want to

people of earth

important and arrive

here with all the birds and

people of earth! people of earth yes

not of any nation

this forest

is not of any nation

people of earth

there can be no people and earth

we have come here as a part of this

we walk in it

we can embrace it with open arms

and find that home here

it is not in a concrete building

those are only your belongings

belong with earth

it is earth your soul calls to

   the idea of a desert

    and the waterfall

all this beautiful wonder of so many springs

that clear etheric water

lifegiving you admire and sip

lifebringing there is belonging

here

there is an earthmagic

it is of beings who

live here

this creation

and all this life

the pineneedle that falls

too creation

and anything you

do with it

feel with it

this is a life part creation

this is magic

these whiskerwinds

of the macrocosm

pick up any shell and say this is a life part creation

now its significance to you

as you hold it in the palm of your hand

or bead it around your neck

the palms are a place of perception

reception

and too these trees we call palms

we can press our palms to them or

sit and see them rustle windwave all this

living motion

it is known that

coconut is especially

healthy to our body and brains

and these trees are ancient long of earth

living and branching

so different

the pineneedle coconut flower

all this life creation

lifesprial soul

all this living creation creating

all the mushroom sprout the fruits

are still living even if picked and

orange

blossom

flowers

this bee

arrival bringing

a blossom bloom

this tree brings

flowers year after year

   from the earth

   and into the air

   too breathing

   orange flowers flutter

   they are like your eyelashes

   these oranges color and

   living spheres

   from the flower tree

   of fruiting wonder that

   is of this land

   its bees come to visit with reverence

oh this beautiful powerful tree

all this living creation

living part air

inter this energy exchange between

   there is such magnitude in

and vast and gems and flowing water

   there is such beauty in

this sun

and rainbow air

be able to walk undisturbed still perceiving

wherever you may be this is earth

you cannot be separated from all the magic

you are light

our starfield is infinite

and all the rainbow

of birds that dance and flutterflip

or flower that heart true

they rise in

all these colors

reflecting in

all this starlight we are one with

shining the sun

reflecting out

bringing such life forth

to our eyes

to our spirit

rainbow

we find such a newness such a growth in this cosmic

dance

imagining this perspective feeling all the motion

flowing all the photon

alive alive waves and

a soaring cosmos to

reach out and touch

to be touched by as

distant white star grows in your mind

the surface of a comet

its heat glowing vapor

trailing into the space it looprings

feel with spiritual presence

translate by

our sense of touch

you are there

can be and are

visiting with your

angelic tribe and now being new

now being free to begin

and anew arrive with empowerment pure

with life clarity

with motivations we harmony

collective utopia of light

   create within

and new newness that glows

like the brightest star

    angelic

and radiating

    radiant

    light

creating all of this newness

may we move positive

and too a light there is bright

bright utopia

we are with angels

in this thought

and so many beings of light

there is true blessing

we find and with us with us

with us

all this love

all this flowing life

of divine radiance

that into sky

the clouds write

it is a

faithful gift and

belief

if we can clairvoyant precognitive transmutative

want to restore

the faith is in knowing

we can

in being empowered against any adversity

in being empowered by adversity

when we are light

and when we are rising truly

restoring this planet with

faith and knowing

this light

there is possibility and this is

we are aware

we will make anew

this flowing realization

flowing this realization

into the present

utopia

and all the lights

there is no illusory authority or false indoctrination

only willing luminescence enlightenment and free

aware unmanipulated

we are not manipulated manipulating

or hateful deceived manipulating

or manipulated hateful or harmful

only a flowing light

sensitive and perceiving

sensitive to these manufactured deceptions

there is no inferior

there is light snd

enlightened

light and

freed

dainty heart

free earth and how beautiful all this is